Fran the Foolish Frankfurter

Level 6 – Orange

Helpful Hints for Reading at Home

The graphemes (written letters) and phonemes (units of sound) used throughout this series are aligned with Letters and Sounds. This offers a consistent approach to learning, whether reading at home or in the classroom.

HERE IS A LIST OF GRAPHEMES FOR THIS PHASE OF LEARNING. AN EXAMPLE OF THE PRONUNCIATION CAN BE FOUND IN BRACKETS.

Phase 5			
ay (day)	ou (out)	ie (tie)	ea (eat)
oy (boy)	ir (girl)	ue (blue)	aw (saw)
wh (when)	ph (photo)	ew (new)	oe (toe)
au (Paul)	a_e (make)	e_e (these)	i_e (like)
o_e (home)	u_e (rule)		

Phase 5 Alternative Pronunciations of Graphemes			
a (hat, what)	e (bed, she)	i (fin, find)	o (hot, so, other)
u (but, unit)	c (cat, cent)	g (got, giant)	ow (cow, blow)
ie (tied, field)	ea (eat, bread)	er (farmer, herb)	ch (chin, school, chef)
y (yes, by, very)	ou (out, shoulder, could, you)		

HERE ARE SOME WORDS WHICH YOUR CHILD MAY FIND TRICKY.

Phase 5 Tricky Words			
oh	their	people	Mr
Mrs	looked	called	asked
could			

TOP TIPS FOR HELPING YOUR CHILD TO READ:

- Allow children time to break down unfamiliar words into units of sound and then encourage children to string these sounds together to create the word.

- Encourage your child to point out any focus phonics when they are used.

- Read through the book more than once to grow confidence.

- Ask simple questions about the text to assess understanding.

- Encourage children to use illustrations as prompts.

This book focuses on /o_e/ and /u_e/ and is an Orange level 6 book band.

Fran the Foolish Frankfurter

Written by
Shalini Vallepur

Illustrated by
Simona Hodonova

Fran dropped things and tripped over all the time. Look out, Fran!

Fran was a klutz. She got called a foolish frankfurter by her pals, her teacher and her mum all the time. But Fran just smiled.

"Fran, you are a foolish frankfurter!" Mum said to Fran one morning.
"I had hoped to make you some toast, Mum," Fran said.

The toast Fran had made for Mum was black and burnt. Fran had tried to make something nice for her mum. Things never went right.

One day, Fran and her pals were playing at the park. Fran went up a tree. She went high up, right to the treetop.
"Fran, what are you doing?" called Fran's pal. "You might fall!"

There was a gust of wind and Fran fell off the treetop. She landed right on her bum.

On a different day, Fran and her pals were playing on the street. It started to rain, but Fran did not have her raincoat.

"Run! Run!" her pals yelled.
"Wait for me!" Fran said. Fran started to run after her pals, but she tripped. She started to weep and her leg started to bleed.

Fran went home. Her feet were wet, and she was sad. "What is the matter, frankfurter?" Mum asked.

"I am sick of being a foolish frankfurter, Mum. I keep getting hurt," said Fran.
"It's fine, Fran," said Mum.

That night, Mum tucked Fran into bed. Mum hugged Fran and drew the sheets up to her chin. "Sleep tight, Fran," Mum said.

"I keep getting hurt and things never go right. I am sick of being a foolish frankfurter," said Fran.

Fran was tucked up tight in bed. She started to drift off into a deep sleep.

When she woke up, Fran tried to get out of bed, but she started to turn.

Fran looked down and saw that she had turned into a frankfurter! And she was not in her bed – she was in a cooking pan! She was having a bad dream.

In a flash, Fran was on the treetop at the park.
"Why am I in the tree?" she said.

There was a bird in the nest that was looking for food. It saw Fran and came closer. "How rude! Ow!" Fran fell off the branch.

Fran was on the street again. She saw her pals running away from the rain. She went to run and jump after them, but she fell over and started to spin. Fran twisted and flopped all the way down the street.

Fran did not stop flopping down the street.
And in fact, Fran hoped she did not stop!

"Weee! This is fun, I want to keep falling!" said Fran. She was spinning, twirling and flipping all the way down the road.

Fran woke up at home with a smile on her face. She looked down to see that she was a person again. She was amazed.

"It was not bad as a frankfurter. I had a lot of fun," said Fran.

The next morning, Mum came down to a shock. There was toast with lots of jam, and a mug of coffee waiting for her.

"Fran, did you make this for me?" asked Mum.
"Yes, I did. I did my best to make it for you, Mum! It is not bad as a frankfurter, just not a foolish one!" said Fran.

"Thank you, frankfurter!" said Mum. She gave Fran a big hug.

Fran the Foolish Frankfurter

1. What did Fran do to the toast she made for Mum?

2. How do you think Fran felt about being clumsy?

3. What does Fran turn into in her bad dream?
   (a) A noodle
   (b) A frankfurter
   (c) A banana

4. What did Fran make for Mum the next morning?

5. What do you think Fran learned from her bad dream? How do you think you would feel if you were Fran?

© This edition published in 2023. First published in 2021.
BookLife Publishing Ltd.
King's Lynn, Norfolk, PE30 4LS, UK

ISBN 978-1-80155-999-7

All rights reserved. Printed in Poland.
A catalogue record for this book is
available from the British Library.

Fran the Foolish Frankfurter
Written by Shalini Vallepur
Illustrated by Simona Hodonova

An Introduction to BookLife Readers...

Our Readers have been specifically created in line with the London Institute of Education's approach to book banding and are phonetically decodable and ordered to support each phase of the Letters and Sounds document.

Each book has been created to provide the best possible reading and learning experience. Our aim is to share our love of books with children, providing both emerging readers and prolific page-turners with beautiful books that are guaranteed to provoke interest and learning, regardless of ability.

BOOK BAND GRADED using the Institute of Education's approach to levelling.

PHONETICALLY DECODABLE supporting each phase of Letters and Sounds.

EXERCISES AND QUESTIONS to offer reinforcement and to ascertain comprehension.

BEAUTIFULLY ILLUSTRATED to inspire and provoke engagement, providing a variety of styles for the reader to enjoy whilst reading through the series.

AUTHOR INSIGHT:
SHALINI VALLEPUR

Passionate about books from a very young age, Shalini Vallepur received the award of Norfolk County Scholar for her outstanding grades. Later on she read English at the University of Leicester, where she stayed to complete her Modern Literature MA. Whilst at university, Shalini volunteered as a Storyteller to help children learn to read, which gave her experience and expertise in the way children pick up and retain information. She used her knowledge and her background and implemented them in the 32 books that she has written for BookLife Publishing. Shalini's writing easily takes us to different worlds, and the serenity and quality of her words are sure to captivate any child who picks up her books.

This book focuses on /o_e/ and /u_e/ and is an Orange level 6 book band.